D0093704

TO:

FROM:

PRAISE FOR DAVID BARDSLEY

"Dr. David Bardsley's workshops and retreats are a great opportunity to better understand your personal capacity to change your life at any age, through attention to the brain's ability to change and grow, as a result of neuroplasticity!"

—LARRY HILES, CEO, TEC Canada

"I needed this to make a change. I am going to take some action now!"

—G. D.

"I heard Dr. Bardsley six months ago, and I added one hour to my sleep and thirty minutes of exercise to my day; now, on hikes, I take the more advanced routes!"

—R. B.

"Totally enjoyed the experience, I feel like I can take control of my health and my life now."

—J. C.

"David is the youngest sixty-nine-year-old I have ever met!"

—NICK MATHESON, Executive Coach

Photo Credits
Internals: page viii © Melpomenem/Getty Images; page xi © Re_sky/Shutterstock; page xii © Freepik; page 3 © Tero Vesalainen/Shutterstock; page 4 © HappyAprilBoy/Shutterstock; page 9 © rawpixel/Unsplash; page 10 © Sean Gladwell/Getty Images; page 13 © Markus Spiske/Unsplash; page 14 © Rostislav Sedlacek/Shutterstock; page 16 © Jeff Sheldon/Unsplash; page 19 © Goh Rhy Yan/Unsplash; page 20 © Petr Malyshev/Shutterstock; page 22 © rawpixel/Unsplash; page 25 © smolaw/Shutterstock; page 26-27 © Austris Augusts/Unsplash; page 28 © Freepik; page 30 © GLYPHstock/Shutterstock; page 33 © Jesse Orrico/Unsplash; page 37 © Anastasiia Moiseieva/Shutterstock; page 39 © Alexey Lin/Unsplash; page 40 © Yeti Studio/Shutterstock; page 42 © Freepik; page 45 © Olyina/Shutterstock; page 49 © ssuaphotos/Shutterstock; page 52 © Chinnapong/Shutterstock; page 55 © Freepik; page 58-59 © Bruno Nascimento/Unsplash; page 60 © Freepik; page 64 © Anne Preble/Unsplash; page 67 © Binh Thanh Bui/Shutterstock; page 68 © Drew Beamer/Unsplash; page 71 © Daniel Padavona/Shutterstock; page 76-77 © Autumn Goodman/Unsplash; page 78 © Tierney MJ/Shutterstock; page 81 © Martin Barak/Unsplash; page 82 © areebarbar/Shutterstock; page 86 © Ilnur Kalimullin/Unsplash; page 89 © Katrina Leigh/Shutterstock; page 91 © Joshua Lanzarini/Unsplash; page 92 © unoL/Shutterstock; page 95 © gopixa/Shutterstock; page 99 © Freepik; page 103 © Todd Diemer/Unsplash; page 105 © Lucas Davies/Unsplash; page 107 © Susan Law Cain/Shutterstock; page 103 © Sydney Rae/Unsplash; page 112-113 © Lindsay Henwood/Unsplash; page 117 © Didecs/Shutterstock; page 118 © Freepik; page 122 © Re_sky/Shutterstock; page 125 © Rebecca Blandon/Unsplash; page 126 © Heder Neves/Unsplash; page 128-129 © Leonard Von Bibra/Unsplash; page 130 © Tierney MJ/Shutterstock; page 133 © Elvira Koneva/Shutterstock; page 134 © Daria Nepriakhina/Unsplash; page 137 © Jared Sluyter/Unsplash

Published by Simple Truths, an imprint of Sourcebooks, Inc.
P.O. Box 4410, Naperville, Illinois 60567-4410
(630) 961-3900
Fax: (630) 961-2168
sourcebooks.com

Library of Congress Cataloging-in-Publication data is on file with the publisher.

Printed and bound in China.
OGP 10 9 8 7 6 5 4 3 2 1

SMARTER NEXT YEAR

THE REVOLUTIONARY SCIENCE FOR A SMARTER, HAPPIER YOU

DR. DAVID C. BARDSLEY

ACKNOWLEDGMENTS

THIS WORK WOULD NEVER HAVE come to fruition without the help and support of Suzanne Balcom, Kim Hunter, Lee Pardee, and the incredible team at Sourcebooks. To these people I owe everything. My heartfelt thanks and grateful appreciation.

TABLE OF CONTENTS

MY WAKE-UP CALL

IT WAS A DARK AND cold Friday afternoon late in November as I drove toward home. I decided to drop by the local supermarket to pick up some groceries for the weekend. The first item on my list was granola, so I made my way to the bulk food section, knowing they had six or seven different types of granola to choose from. For those unfamiliar with how a bulk food section in a grocery store works, let me explain. Each food item is in a separate bin, and each bin has its own five-digit identification number, which is necessary for the cashier to enter at checkout. I selected the granola, scooped it into the plastic bag, attached the identification tag, and then looked for the pen to write down the identification number. Someone had taken the pen. *No big deal,* I thought. *It is only a five-digit number. I can certainly remember a five-digit number.*

I repeated the number to myself. *86372, 86372, 86372, 86372, got it.* I threw the granola into my cart and continued shopping. Fifteen minutes later, I was ready to check out, but it was a Friday afternoon and there were huge lines. I eventually made my way up to the cashier. She was a young girl and very impatient. Without even looking up, she grabbed my grocery items and started scanning them rapidly. When she picked up the granola and looked for the identifying bin number, I said, "I'm sorry. I didn't write the number on the granola because someone had taken the pen, but the bin number is 867... 8763... 87623... No, 86723!"

As I fumbled trying to remember the number, I

heard someone at the back of the line whisper, "He's having a senior moment." Everybody chuckled. Except for me. I did not chuckle, I could not chuckle, because I found myself in a state of shock. Not only had I forgotten a simple series of numbers, I was completely humiliated. To make matters worse, just two weeks prior I had sat beside my mother in the psychiatrist office as she received the devastating diagnosis: Alzheimer's. I was clearly worried for her future and my own.

After I left the grocery store and got into my car,

I just sat there for a few moments thinking to myself, *What just happened in there? I am fifty-eight years old. How could I possibly be having a senior moment?*

Well, that was my wake-up call, my epiphany, my *aha!* moment! The very next day, I started my eleven-year intensive research into what causes these so-called senior moments—the decline in cognitive ability—and what can be done about it. What I discovered was truly amazing and transformative for me. During the course of my research, I came across countless stories of others who dramatically changed the trajectory of their lives by understanding and applying the principles provided in this book. I now travel throughout North America presenting this information in seminars more than sixty times per year. The intention of this book is to share that transformative information with you.

The popular understanding of cognitive ability and its decline—cognitive impairment—is full of myths and misconceptions. In the chapters that follow, we will debunk many of those myths. The chief myth that we will dispel is that we are born with a certain amount of intelligence, which we inherit from our parents, and that amount of intelligence remains fixed and can never be increased throughout our lifetimes. I am going to present you with the latest scientific information and the evidence-based best practices for improving our cognitive abilities at any stage of life, whether we are 6, 66, or 106.

But before we dive in, I'd like to define some key terminology I will be using throughout the book:

COGNITIVE ABILITY: the brain's ability to preform various tasks, such as learning, memory, attention, deduction, and concentration. Knowledge is the end result of these tasks.

NEURON: the primary brain cell associated with intelligence. Humans have one hundred million of these cells and each cell has ten thousand branches connecting it to other brain cells. This makes up our neural network.

NEUROTRANSMITTER: chemicals which transmit the electrical signal across the tiny space between neurons. (Neurons never physically touch one another so they rely on neurotransmitters to transmit the electrical signal.)

EXECUTIVE FUNCTION: an umbrella term for the neurologically based skills involving mental control and self-regulation. It simply refers to a list of abilities (refer to the box below) people who we deem to be very clever seem to possess. These abilities are considered to be the higher order of the human intellect. This is what truly sets us apart from the other primates.

LIST OF EXECUTIVE FUNCTIONS

- Goal setting
- Flexibility
- Inhibiting
- Executing
- Organizing
- Problem solving
- Pacing
- Sequencing
- Initiating
- Using feedback
- Self-monitoring
- Generalizing
- Shifting
- Prioritizing
- Planning

YOU WERE GIVEN YOUR GENES, BUT WHAT YOU DO WITH THEM IS UP TO YOU.

—David Bardsley

Travel is to make a journey or to have an adventure to somewhere by bicycle, train, airplane, car, motorcycle, or boat. It could be an exploration to somewhere new planned or unplanned to meet new people, new things and new places. There are different types of adventures waiting for you to explore.

There are lots of places to explore. Places could be urban or suburban. Some people loves to be with nature to free their minds and refresh their souls, but some like to be in the city. You will get lots of benefits such as exploring new culture.

CHAPTER 1
INTELLIGENCE

I AM GOING TO ASK you to take a few moments and reflect on your own life. See if you can identify the time of your peak mental ability, meaning the time period when your cognitive powers were at their best. When you could take in large amounts of new information quickly, understanding it easily. When your recall was fast, sharp, and accurate. For some of you, it may be right now, at this current time in your life, but others often point to some time in the past. Many say it was perhaps their high school years or their college years. Certainly, those are times in our lives when we made a great deal of effort to take in a large amount of information in a relatively short period of time, but it is not necessarily the time of our peak cognitive abilities. In fact, the human brain does not fully mature until we are into our mid- to late-twenties.

When you ask people to identify the time in their lives when they were in their best physical conditions, most people have no problem answering. In fact, they usually admit it was some time in the past, often very far back in the past. They will often regale you with stories of the good old glory days of their physical prowess.

Conversely, I find that most people do not like to admit they are not as smart as they used to be. Or if they will admit there has been a decrease in brain power, they often attribute that to the aging process. We assume that as we get older, our cognitive abilities slowly start to erode. The good news is that all the latest neuroscience is telling us there should be no decrease in our cognitive abilities—none whatsoever— until we are into our seventies and eighties, and even

then it is not inevitable. Any decrease that does occur before this is often due to a very pervasive condition called mild cognitive impairment (MCI), which we will speak a great deal about in the following chapters.

I promise not to bore you with a lot of biochemistry or neuroanatomy, but it is critically important for you to understand what chemical processes take place in your brain on a daily basis—related to your intelligence—that you have a great deal of control over. If you were to look up the definition of intelligence in a series of dictionaries, you would find slightly differing definitions, but they all basically boil down to this:

INTELLIGENCE:
the ability to take in
new information, understand
that information, store it,
retrieve it, and then use it in
some meaningful way.

In 1983, the psychologist Howard Gardner put forward his theory of multiple intelligences, which is now the most widely accepted intelligence theory. In his book *Frames of Mind: The Theory of Multiple Intelligences*, Gardner claims there is not one intelligence, rather there are eight separate and distinct intelligences, and each one of us possesses all eight of these intelligences at varying levels. Here are the eight intelligence categories explained in detail:

1. LOGICAL/MATHEMATICAL

This intelligence has as much to do with pattern recognition, abstract thinking, and overall imagination as it does with our ability to manipulate complex numbers and equations. People with logical/mathematical intelligence are good at scientific investigations and identifying relationships between different things. They are also good at understanding complex and abstract ideas. People in this category are often best suited for the following professions: accountant, auditor, bookkeeper, computer analyst, computer programmer, computer technician, database designer, detective, economist, engineer, lawyer, mathematician, network analyst, pharmacist, physician, researcher, and scientist statistician.

2. SPATIAL

This refers to our ability to see things in a third dimension that do not already exist. A sculptor does not just see a large block of marble in front of her, she actually sees the shape inside the block that she has

to create. Architects have exceptionally good spatial intelligence. They are able to look at a flat two-dimensional drawing and visualize exactly what it will look like in a third dimension. People in this category are often best suited for these professions: architect, artist, computer programmer, engineer, film animator, graphic artist, interior decorator, mechanic, navigator, outdoor guide, photographer, pilot, sculptor, strategic planner, surveyor, three-dimensional modeler, truck driver, urban planner, and webmaster.

3. LINGUISTIC

This involves our ability to use sounds and tones to connote meaning. If we take a group of individuals at any age and teach them a first, second, or third language all at the same pace, certain individuals will pick up the new languages much faster than others because of their high linguistic intelligence. Knowing and understanding nuances of a language is also indicative of a higher linguistic intelligence. No matter how many terabytes of memory or how fast the RAM processing speed, there is not a computer on this planet that can make a joke. There is not a computer that understands sarcasm. These are considered nuances of a language, and knowing, understanding, and being able to use them is indicative of a higher linguistic intelligence. People in this category are often best suited for these professions: attorney, comedian, communications specialist, curator, editor in publishing, historian, journalist, language translator, librarian, marketing consultant, newscaster, poet, politician, songwriter, speech writer, talk-show host, teacher, and writer.

4. BODILY-KINESTHETIC

This intelligence deals with our ability to move our bodies through time and space. Athletes and dancers exhibit a high kinesthetic intelligence. The ability to use our bodies to manipulate other objects in time and space is also indicative of a high bodily-kinesthetic intelligence. The juggler with six balls going in the air at the

same time is a good example of this type of intelligence, as is a surgeon with his or her precision scalpel. People in this category are often best suited for these professions: actor, athlete, carpenter, dancer, dentist, firefighter, forest ranger, jeweler, mechanic, personal trainer, physical education teacher, physical therapist, recreation specialist, sports doctor, surgeon, video game designer, and yoga instructor.

5. MUSICAL

If we were to take a group of individuals, of any age, teach them some musical theory, and allow them to practice for exactly the same length of time, some of those individuals would be far more accomplished on the instrument than others. People with musical intelligence appear to have an enhanced sensitivity to rhythm, pitch, meter, tone, and melody. People in this category are often best suited for these professions: audiologist, choir director, music conductor, music teacher, musician, piano tuner, recording engineer, singer, songwriter, sound editor, and voice actor.

6. INTERPERSONAL

The cornerstone of interpersonal intelligence is empathy. Empathy is our ability to be in tune with the feelings and needs of others without them necessarily expressing those to us verbally. Interpersonal intelligence is often referred to as emotional intelligence, emotional quotient (EQ) versus intelligence quotient (IQ). Emotional intelligence can be tested for, and study after study has repeatedly shown that a high score on the emotional intelligence rating is a much better indicator of how successful a student will be through his or her four years of college than a high score on their SAT exams. Typically, all great managers and all great sales people have high emotional intelligence. People with high interpersonal intelligence are skilled verbal and nonverbal communicators. People in this category are often best suited for these professions: actor, administrator, communications specialist, conflict resolution specialist, customer service rep, dental hygienist, group mediator, human resources manager, manager,

marketing specialist, nurse, Peace Corps participant, politician, psychologist, religious leader, salesperson, social director, social worker, teacher, trainer facilitator, travel counselor, and waiter/waitress.

7. INTRAPERSONAL

This intelligence refers to our ability to understand ourselves. Intrapersonal intelligence allows us to know and understand our strengths and weaknesses and predict how we would react if we were put in any given set of circumstances. People in this category are often best suited for these professions: actor, artist, career counselor, consultant, criminologist, entrepreneur, energy healer, futurist or trend predictor, intelligence officer, personal counselor, philosopher, program planner, psychic, psychologist, researcher, small business owner, spiritual counselor, theologian, therapist, writer, and wellness counselor.

8. NATURALISTIC

This intelligence refers to our innate ability to be in tune with nature and our environments. Perhaps you have a neighbor living beside you in an identical house. You have the same lawn, the same garden. Their garden looks terrific, yours does not look so good. So you ask them, "What are you doing that is different?" You find out you have exactly the same soil, you are using the same seeds and the same fertilizer. You are watering on the same schedule, and you have the same amount of sunshine. Yet their garden looks great and yours does not. When asked, they are unable to explain the reason for this. What we often say is those people have a "green thumb." What those people actually have is a high naturalistic intelligence. They seem to just know what is necessary and when regarding nature. Perhaps a little less water here or a little more water there. Perhaps less sunshine in one area and more in another. They seem to recognize when the vegetation is not thriving and have an innate knowledge of what is necessary to correct the problem. People in this category are often best suited for these professions: air quality specialist, animal health technician, anthropologist, astronomer, biologist, botanist, dog trainer, environmental lawyer, farmer, forest ranger, gardener, geologist, landscaper, meteorologist, nature photographer, park naturalist, veterinarian assistant, water conservationist, wetlands ecologist, wilderness doctor, wilderness guide, and wildlife illustrator.

In our flawed school system, children from an early age are given a series of standardized tests that determine their relative strengths and weaknesses. An inordinate amount of time is then spent focusing on the child's weaknesses, trying to bring them up to some arbitrary standard of proficiency. Instead, the focus should be on the child's natural strengths and talents and placing the majority of our efforts nurturing and developing those.

The same is true for adults. Do not waste a large amount of time and effort focusing on your cognitive weaknesses, the things you naturally struggle with. Rather, identify your strengths and direct the majority

"YOUR PRESENT CIRCUMSTANCES
DON'T DETERMINE WHERE YOU
CAN GO; THEY MERELY DETERMINE
WHERE YOU START."

—Nido Qubein

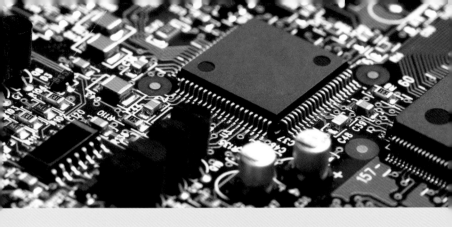

of your efforts improving and growing those areas. Not only will you see enhancement rapidly, it will be infinitely more enjoyable. For more than a century, neuroscience believed that the brain was hardwired. The generally accepted thinking was that the brain works on electrical circuitry, and neuroscience believed that once those circuits formed—which they do very early in our infancy and childhood—they were permanent. Each circuit would then control a specific aspect of our mental and physical functioning. They were "hardwired" much the same as the electrical circuits in your home are. No matter how many times you flip the light switch on and off in your foyer, the light in the upstairs bathroom is never going to turn on, because your home is hardwired.

It was believed for hundreds of years that we inherited all our intelligence from our parents. We now know this is false. We only inherit 50 percent, the other 50 percent is developmental; how rich and stimulating our environment is as infants and small children. Until thirty years ago, it was believed that by age eight or nine our intelligence was fixed because it was hardwired. It would remain the same until our senior years when it would begin to decline.

But all of that changed thirty years ago with the discovery of neuroplasticity, which has revolutionized neuroscience. Since that time, there have been many neuroplastic pioneers who deserve a great deal of recognition, each of their discoveries lent another layer to our understanding of the brain's tremendous ability to change itself and our cognitive intelligence. Your brain, including all of your cognitive strengths and weaknesses, is *changeable*.

CHAPTER 2
MILD COGNITIVE IMPAIRMENT

WHAT I HAVE BEEN REFERRING to as "senior moments" can also be medically defined as symptoms for mild cognitive impairment (MCI), which is simply an overall decrease in the areas of cognitive functioning such as memory, language, thinking, and judgment. Meaning, these "senior moments" can add up to be a significant concern for early onset of Alzheimer's disease or dementia. The majority of people over forty in the western world are certainly not aging healthily and find themselves living in fear of such signs of decline.

According to the Center for Disease Control (CDC), 50 percent of the population start to exhibit some symptoms of mild cognitive impairment (MCI) by age forty. That's right Baby Boomers and Gen Xers, by age *forty*. Clearly understand they are not saying that 50 percent of the population by age forty have diagnosable MCI, rather that they exhibit some of the signs.

What are some signs or symptoms in our everyday lives that would indicate some degree of MCI? Most but not all will involve memory—"senior moments." It is not that memory is necessarily the first thing that starts slipping, it is just one of the first things that we notice when it does start to slip—like my "senior moment" in the supermarket.

EXAMPLES OF MILD COGNITIVE IMPAIRMENT

Here is a list of common everyday occurrences that are related to mild cognitive impairment that most of us can identify with. Although these symptoms pop up from time to time, the real warning sign is when they are occurring with increasing frequency.

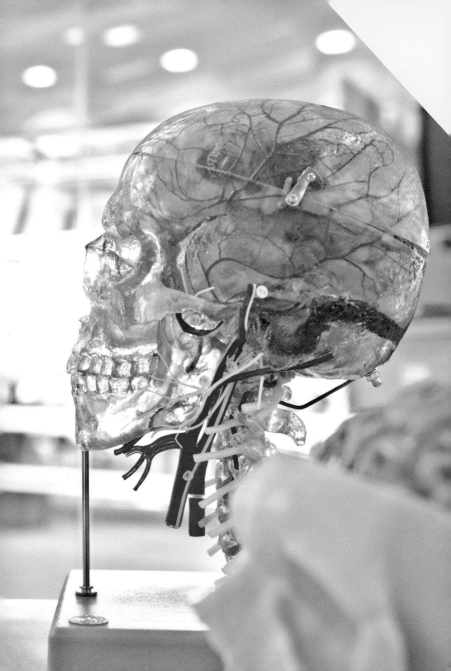

1. TRAIN OF THOUGHT

We lose our train of thought while telling a story, reading a book, or watching a movie. We totally forget the story line, punch line, or plot. How often have you been talking to someone and all of a sudden you go totally blank?

2. DATES AND EVENTS

We find we forget important dates and events, so we have to write them down. We have to diarize them, put them in a calendar, or enter them on our phone with a reminder.

3. OBJECTS

Suddenly, we find ourselves forgetting objects and details more frequently. We lose our keys, cell phones, and glasses, and we forget where the car is in the parking lot.

4. DIRECTIONS

You have trouble finding your way around environments with which you have some familiarity. Perhaps you have been to that store or that restaurant once or twice before, and now you are having trouble finding your way back.

5. INFORMATION

I realize this is the information age, and we are inundated with new and fast-changing information daily. However, we find we still cannot process the same volume of information that we once did. Perhaps you feel increasingly overwhelmed by making decisions, planning steps to accomplish a task, or interpreting instructions.

6. IMPULSIVITY

Since we do not process information as quickly as we once did, we often become frustrated.

It may seem that there is just too much information to weigh and consider in order to make the correct decisions. Overwhelmed, we impulsively make choices instead of weighing choices properly.

7. OTHERS NOTICE

If you were to gain a pound a year for fifteen years, you would not notice it. However, if you run into an old friend who hasn't seen you in fifteen years, he or she would certainly notice, and he or she might even say something about it. The same can be said about symptoms of mental decline. While they may not be obvious to you, if someone does have the courage to point something like this out to you, please do not get angry with them and do not go into denial, because they are actually doing you a favor.

MCI-related issues may get a little worse over time and then just stop and never progress any further for the rest of your life. However, the same issues may progressively get worse as time goes on and result in dementia or Alzheimer's disease. Not every person with MCI will end up with a dementia, but what we do know is that 100 percent of individuals with dementia and Alzheimer's disease started with minor MCI issues. That is why it is so critical to identify what is happening and reverse it during its earliest stages.

IT IS THE SAME WITH
PEOPLE AS IT IS WITH RIDING
A BIKE. ONLY WHEN MOVING
CAN ONE COMFORTABLY
MAINTAIN ONE'S BALANCE.

—Albert Einstein

CHAPTER 3

COMMON CAUSES OF MILD COGNITIVE IMPAIRMENT

IT IS IMPORTANT FOR YOU to understand the causes of mild cognitive impairment (MCI) so you can address them. In some cases, this will involve simply stopping a negative activity that you are already doing that leads to or exacerbates MCI. In other cases, it will involve initiating a new activity that will lead to a decrease in MCI and a corresponding increase in your cognitive ability. Below are the catalysts for MCI and a few ways you can avoid or combat them:

SLEEP DEPRIVATION

With rare exception, adults need seven to nine hours of sleep per night. I am sure we all know individuals who claim they get by just fine on five or six hours of sleep. That is just what they are doing—getting by. They are not performing at their cognitive best. Teenagers need from nine to eleven hours of sleep a night, but the average American high school student gets only six and a half hours of sleep per night. I cannot emphasize how important sleep is to your cognitive ability and mental functioning.

Testing the amount of cognitive decline that occurs with sleep deprivation is not difficult. Studies have shown that if a group of military personnel is administered a cognitive test, then deprived so they receive only six or less hours of sleep for five consecutive nights, and then retested, they show a 60 percent decrease in their test scores.

At one time, neuroscience believed we needed to sleep because our brains needed to rest. We now know this is completely false. The latest generation of medical imaging devices like functional magnetic resonance imaging (fMRI), positron emission tomography (PET), and single proton emitting computerized tomography (SPECT) scans allow us to take a video of the brain while it is working. They reveal that your brain is actually far more active while you are sleeping than while you are awake. Specifically, they show that the asleep brain only exhibits less electrical activity than the awake brain 20 percent of the time. The other 80 percent of the time you're asleep, your brain is crackling with chemical and bioelectrical energy. While we are sleeping, our brains review all the information that our five senses took in while we were awake. It sorts, assimilates, compartmentalizes, and stores the information for future recall. It is now believed that if we did not sleep at all, we would not have any permanent memories formed. Students, take note: The best way to transfer the information you are studying into long-term memory is to go to sleep immediately after studying.

At times we are asked to make a decision on something and we are not sure how to respond, so we often say, "Let me sleep on it." When you awake in the morning, you have some clarity on the issue, because your brain has been hard at work while you slept.

If you follow these four simple steps, you can be assured of a significant improvement in the duration and quality of your sleep:

1. **TURN DOWN THE THERMOSTAT.** Studies have shown there is an optimum room temperature for sleep, which is 60 to 66 degrees Fahrenheit (15 to 19 degrees Celsius). If you

are like me and do not like getting out of bed when the room is 60 degrees, then invest in a programmable thermostat, and set it so the room temperature will rise to 70 degrees twenty minutes before you wake up for the day.

2. SET THREE ALARMS.

a. Awake alarm—the time you want to get up in the morning (6:00 a.m.).

b. Sleep alarm—the time you want to go to bed. This should be set eight hours before the awake alarm (10:00 p.m.).

c. Preparation alarm—this alarm signals that it is time to start getting ready to go to

bed. It is set thirty minutes before the sleep alarm (9:30 p.m.). Put on your pajamas, brush your teeth, finish up any projects, etc. Most importantly, it is time to turn off *all* screens: computer, television, video games, cell phones, etc. All light waves—particularly blue light (screens)—decrease the production of melatonin, which is a hormone produced by your brain that helps you fall asleep and stay asleep. Melatonin is produced in response to darkness, so make the room as dark as possible to ensure maximum melatonin production.

3. TAKE MELATONIN SUPPLEMENTS. Most pharmacologic sleep aids are chemicals that your body does not recognize or produce. In most cases, neuroscience cannot explain how they induce or maintain sleep. As previously mentioned, melatonin is a hormone that your body naturally produces. Like many hormones, melatonin production generally decreases with age. When you take melatonin as a sleep aid, you are giving your body something it already produces. Melatonin is available (without a prescription) in any store that sells vitamins. It comes in 3–10 mg tablets. Start with the smallest dose and work your way up if needed. Rarely, people describe "strange" dreams when taking melatonin supplements. These almost always disappear when the dosage is reduced.

4. **TRY GUIDED MEDITATION OR AUDIO-BOOKS.** Listening to the direction found in a guided meditation or audiobook engages your brain and does not allow you to think those random, ruminating, negative thoughts that keep you from falling asleep or returning to sleep if you wake up in the middle of the night. I find audiobooks particularly helpful, because

you can set a timer that turns the book off in fifteen or twenty minutes (or whatever time you want) so it is not playing all night while you are asleep. Chances are your parents read you stories to help you fall asleep when you were a child. Why should it be any different now that you are an adult? Audiobooks can be purchased online or borrowed from your local library. Almost all libraries have audiobooks—all you need is a library card. You can download the files to your phone or computer, and they will expire in a communicated time frame.

TOXIC EXPOSURES

Our environment—including the atmosphere, the soil, and the food we ingest on a daily basis—is full of toxins. We cannot eliminate these toxins from our environment, but we need to try the best we can to reduce our exposure to them. Almost all pesticides are neurotoxins, no matter which company produces them. Pesticides work by destroying the nervous system of the insects they protect crops from. However, humans also ingest these toxins on a daily basis through our food sources, and we have no idea what level of consumption is safe regarding cognitive health. We only know the level at which a disease, conditions, or *hard symptoms* develop. A hard symptom in medicine is something that is observable. A pain in your elbow

would be a hard symptom. These neurotoxins build up in our systems daily without us knowing, until a tipping point is reached, and a hard symptom of condition appears. The untested scope for all neurotoxins would be found in soft symptoms, but unfortunately such symptoms are nearly impossible to monitor for brain functionality. Therefore, neurotoxins may be slowly eroding our cognitive ability without us realizing it until a critical point is reached, and it becomes obvious something is wrong. While there is also the chance that they may be doing no damage whatsoever, why would you jeopardize your mental facilities without proof one way or another?

The point I am trying to make here is not to scare you but rather to arm you with questions to ask so you can develop plans to limit exposure. The fact remains that we are surrounded by these neurotoxins. It is impossible to escape them all, but we need to try our best to reduce our exposure to them.

Look around your home and workplace. Are there

open or leaking containers of solvents, paint, turpentine, gasoline, insecticides, or cleaning products? I am not saying you should never use these products. What I am saying is read the warnings on the labels and follow the directions. When it says, *Use in a well-ventilated area*, make sure you do. The manufacturers are telling you that for a reason. The fumes can be neurotoxic. If it suggests you use a respirator, make sure you do. One of the fastest ways to get a substance into your brain is through your nose. That is why people snort drugs. Make sure you are not inadvertently "snorting" neurotoxins.

PSYCHIATRIC DISORDERS

Very few people are brave enough to talk about their psychiatric problems. We all know individuals who seem to enjoy telling us about their latest physical sickness or hospitalization or even who brag about how many screws and plates they have in the leg they fractured skiing. However, not many people will say to you, "Do

you have a few minutes? I would like to talk about my depression [or anxiety or stress]."

Stress floods your body with two hormones. One is *cortisol*. An excessive amount of this hormone will cause die back, or shrinkage between the branches that connect one brain cell (neuron) to another. This inhibits the electrical signal from passing from one neuron to the next, resulting in slower brain speeds. Stress also floods your body with *adrenaline*. If you are being chased down an alley by a large angry dog, you want your body to produce all the adrenaline it can. Adrenaline is a vasoconstrictor—it reduces blood flow to all your major organs, including your brain. This makes more blood and oxygen available for the skeletal muscles, so you can escape the angry dog. This is the classic fight-or-flight response. When you reach the end of the alley and climb over the fence, the threat is over, and your body stops pumping out adrenaline. This is how the system is supposed to work. Humans, however, do not have to be chased by an angry dog or physically threatened in any way to produce a stress response. We are the only known animals that can elicit a massive physiological stress response just by thinking. All stress is caused by thinking negative thoughts. If you find yourself awake in the middle of the night and cannot return to sleep, it is often because you are ruminating over negative thoughts and experiencing a stress response.

During a period of chronic stress, the adrenaline production continues unabated, and this leads to a chronic decrease in blood flow and oxygen to the brain. The end result is cognitive impairment. There are many excellent books on the subject of preventing and lessening chronic stress. I would strongly recommend that everyone familiarize themselves with some of these techniques and practice them on a daily basis! Here are four of my favorites:

1. **VOLUNTEER.** Studies have shown that service to others has a very beneficial effect in lowering stress levels. I am not talking about writing a check to your favorite charity (however, please continue to do that). I am talking about volunteering your valuable time to help the less fortunate. This produces huge benefits for you and them. When we create an emotional bond with others, our brain releases the hormone *oxytocin*. It is frequently referred to as the "love" hormone because it increases social bonding. Very large amounts are released during child birth and it is responsible for the extremely

strong mother-child bonding. Cortisol levels are driven down when oxytocin levels rise. Volunteering to assist others increases your oxytocin levels and decreases your stress.

2. GUIDED MEDITATION AND IMAGERY. The human brain is not capable of holding two thoughts at the same time (happy and sad thoughts cannot occur simultaneously). I find meditation and imagery much easier and more beneficial if guided by the voice of another. There are many apps (some free) that help

greatly. The most popular include Headspace, Calm, Buddhify, and Meditation Timer.

3. **NEGATIVE THOUGHT REDUCTION.** This involves recognizing negative thoughts (which are the cause of all stress) by counting them and then reframing those thoughts to lessen the stress. The first step is to recognize how many negative thoughts you have. This is best done by counting them. I use the free app Clicker Counter. Each time you have a negative thought, tap the + button. This will make you more aware of your negative thoughts, and the next step is to "reframe" or alter them.

4. **EXERCISE.** Particularly, aerobic exercise is beneficial. This is by far your single biggest weapon in the war against stress. It will be discussed in detail in later chapters.

OVERMEDICATING

A recent study showed the cost of drugs purchased in the United States in the year 2010. Topping the list was the statin Lipitor with a total expenditure of $7.2 billion. A second statin, Crestor, accounted for an expenditure of $3.8 billion. Statins are drugs used to lower cholesterol levels; among the many side effects reported by the manufacturers of these drugs are memory loss and confusion, yet their use is prevalent. Statins are the most prescribed drugs in the world; according to the Centers for Disease Control and Prevention (CDC), one in four American adults takes a statin on a daily basis.

The vast majority of people with high cholesterol are overweight, and many of these people also have high blood pressure, so they are put on antihypertensives. Beta blockers, such as Inderal and Betaloc, are the most commonly used antihypertensive. The manufacturers list mental confusion, depression, and dizziness as some of the possible side effects.

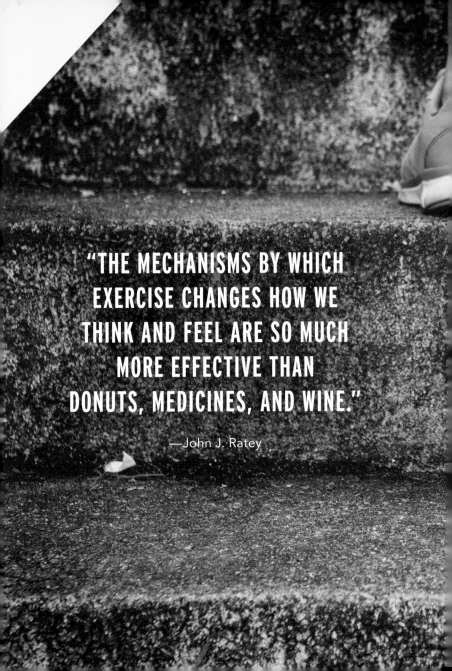

"THE MECHANISMS BY WHICH EXERCISE CHANGES HOW WE THINK AND FEEL ARE SO MUCH MORE EFFECTIVE THAN DONUTS, MEDICINES, AND WINE."

—John J. Ratey

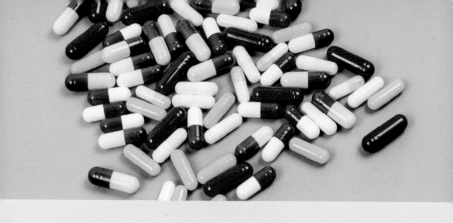

Many of those suffering from high blood pressure and high cholesterol are also placed on anticoagulants to prevent heart attack and stroke. In 2010, the second most costly drug in the United States was Plavix, which had a total expenditure of $6.1 billion. Once again, the manufacturers list mental confusion and disorientation as possible side effects.

According to the CDC, one in four Americans will suffer at least one major bout of depression in their lives for which they will be medicated. The antidepressants Abilify and Seroquel also made the list of the ten most costly drugs in 2010, coming in at $4.6 and $4.4 billion, respectively. Among the many side effects of these medications, the manufacturers list agitation, suicide, and disturbances in speech and language. When you see these warnings, it is not because the drugs affect the muscles of the lips and tongue. It is because they affect the area of the brain responsible for speech and language.

Those of you who have seen the movie or read the book *The Perfect Storm* might remember how the perfect storm developed. There were three separate low-pressure storms off the northeastern Atlantic Coast. Each of these storms by itself was significant, but none were extreme. However, when all three came together—at the same place and at the same time—the resulting superstorm was horrific and deadly. In a similar manner, we see many individuals today who are overweight with high cholesterol and high blood pressure who are taking two, three, or even four of these medications at the same time—all of which have cognitive side effects. It is a perfect cognitive storm waiting to happen. Unfortunately, we do not have many good studies demonstrating the cumulative cognitive effects of multiple medications. Your goal should be to get off of all medications that are not absolutely essential.

You need to team up with your doctor to do this safely. Try to reduce and eventually eliminate medications one at a time. You were placed on the medications for a reason. You will need to explain to your physician what lifestyle changes (exercise, diet, stress relief, etc.) you are going to implement that will allow you to be weaned off the medications. You need to have a plan and you have to put that plan into action. No physician is going to reduce your medications until you make the necessary lifestyle changes. Do not just stop the medications on your own, as this can be very dangerous.

VITAMIN DEFICIENCIES

Many people believe vitamin deficiencies only occur in second- and third-world countries. Nothing could be

further from the truth. There are many vitamin deficiencies in North America and other parts of the Western world. To start with, our food is so highly processed, there is frequently little nutritive value remaining. We can also bring about vitamin deficiencies in our own bodies without even realizing it. One of the more common deficiencies is pernicious anemia, which is caused by lack of vitamin B12. All the B vitamins—particularly B12—are absolutely crucial for the health and proper functioning of our brains and central nervous systems.

When food containing vitamin B12 reaches our stomachs, the B12 is not capable of crossing the lining of the stomach or intestine and entering the bloodstream to be circulated throughout the body. It must first join up with a molecule of a substance called intrinsic factor. Together the molecule of B12 and intrinsic factor form a complex, which is then able to cross the lining of the stomach or intestine and be absorbed into the bloodstream for distribution throughout the body.

Intrinsic factor is produced by specialized cells called *parietal cells*, which line the stomach wall. These cells also produce gastric acid. Unfortunately, many individuals suffer from gastric acid reflux or indigestion. This is frequently caused by an excess of gastric acid in the stomach and a weakening of the sphincter between the stomach and esophagus.

The gastric acid is also produced by the same parietal cells that line the wall of the stomach and produce the intrinsic factor. Many of those individuals suffering from gastric acid reflux or indigestion simply go to the pharmacy and buy off-the-shelf medications with no prescription required. The most popular of these medications are known as proton pump inhibitors. You may recognize some by their brand names such as Prilosec, Prevacid, Nexium, Zegerid. These drugs work very well at reducing the amount of gastric acid produced by the parietal cells. This is wonderful news for the gastric acid reflux sufferer. However, they not only shut down the production of gastric acid, they

also shut down the production of intrinsic factor.

Now, no matter how rich your diet is in vitamin B12, it will simply pass right through the stomach and intestines and come out the lower end. It does not get absorbed into the bloodstream and distributed throughout the body, resulting in pernicious anemia. Two of the most common side effects of pernicious anemia are tingling in the fingers and toes and memory loss. Once the condition is diagnosed, monthly injections of vitamin B12 are often necessary, as this bypasses the malabsorption route. The tingling usually can be reversed, but often the memory loss cannot. Do not confuse proton pump inhibitors with antacids like Tums, Mylanta, or Rolaids. These are not proton pump inhibitors and do not decrease the production of excess gastric acid. They are alkaline substances that work by neutralizing the gastric acid. It is now recommended that if you are taking a proton pump inhibitor (on a daily basis for over a year) you should have your vitamin B12 levels checked on a regular basis.

Intri   also shut down the

parie   Now, no matte

also   B12, it will simply p

uals   intestines and com

is fre   get absorbed into

stom   throughout the bo

the s   Two of the most c

T   anemia are tingling

parie   loss. Once the con

prod   tions of vitamin

suffe   bypasses the malal

go to   can be reversed, b

with   Do not confuse pr

these   like Tums, Mylanta

itors.   pump inhibitors an

such   excess gastric acic

drug: work by neutralizir

acid   mended that if you

news   (on a daily basis fc

not o   vitamin B12 levels

roduction of intrinsic factor.

how rich your diet is in vitamin

ss right through the stomach and

out the lower end. It does not

he bloodstream and distributed

y, resulting in pernicious anemia.

mmon side effects of pernicious

the fingers and toes and memory

ition is diagnosed, monthly injec-

2 are often necessary, as this

orption route. The tingling usually

t often the memory loss cannot.

on pump inhibitors with antacids

or Rolaids. These are not proton

do not decrease the production of

They are alkaline substances that

the gastric acid. It is now recom-

re taking a proton pump inhibitor

over a year) you should have your

ecked on a regular basis.

further from the truth. There are many vitamin deficiencies in North America and other parts of the Western world. To start with, our food is so highly processed, there is frequently little nutritive value remaining. We can also bring about vitamin deficiencies in our own bodies without even realizing it. One of the more common deficiencies is pernicious anemia, which is caused by lack of vitamin B12. All the B vitamins—particularly B12—are absolutely crucial for the health and proper functioning of our brains and central nervous systems.

When food containing vitamin B12 reaches our stomachs, the B12 is not capable of crossing the lining of the stomach or intestine and entering the bloodstream to be circulated throughout the body. It must first join up with a molecule of a substance called intrinsic factor. Together the molecule of B12 and intrinsic factor form a complex, which is then able to cross the lining of the stomach or intestine and be absorbed into the bloodstream for distribution throughout the body.

plus most of our diets change from day to day and therefore nutrition fluctuates. For this reason, I recommend we all take a quality multimineral/vitamin daily.

ALCOHOL

There are many theories about the effect of alcohol on the brain. Although the theories differ, it has been proven that if you add just one drop of alcohol—even if it is diluted—to brain cells in a petri dish, the cells immediately shrivel up and die. We cannot say with certainty the same thing happens inside our brains after we drink alcohol. As of yet, we have no way of placing a miniature microscope inside the brain to observe the direct effects of alcohol. However, there have been many studies over the years showing the debilitated cognitive effects of daily alcohol consumption. In January 2014, the *Journal of Neurology* published a large-scale study with the following conclusion: people who consume more than two-and-a-half drinks per day on a regular basis have a significant increase in cognitive impairment. They defined one drink as one ounce of alcohol, three ounces of wine, or one beer. If we were to read between the lines, they are saying that yes, you can come home from work and have your one nice martini you look forward to all day to unwind. And sure, you can have that seven-ounce glass of wine with your meal...you just can't have three and maintain a healthy life and mind. And no, you can't abstain Monday through Friday and then triple up on the weekend; impact doesn't roll over—it's immediate. Each person has a different capacity to detoxify alcohol. One hundred percent of the alcohol you consume goes first to your liver, where it is chemically broken down and excreted in your urine. It will not reach your brain. However, if you consume more alcohol than your liver can break down, some of it will pass unchanged into your bloodstream, and in 30 seconds or less it will enter your brain, and you will feel the effect (or rather, the buzz).

TRAUMA

The latest reports on mild cumulative head trauma are truly frightening. While you may not think trauma applies to you, you may need to think again. All of the latest studies are showing that you do not have to be knocked unconscious to show a sign of a concussion or have permanent brain damage from mild repetitive head trauma. It can be as simple as heading the ball in soccer, and this results from not only the once or twice the child gets to head the ball during the game; it results from the hundreds of times he or she does it in practice as well.

Mild repetitive head trauma is turning out to be similar to repetitive skin damage from solar radiation. You do not see many six- or seven-year-olds walking around with skin cancer, do you? This is due to the fact that we are all constantly exposed to ultraviolet radiation from the sun, and this starts at a very early age, so the effects take a long time to surface. While the skin repairs 99.9 percent of that damage, there is always a small amount of residual damage. This residual damage adds up year after year, decade after decade, until it finally reaches a critical tipping point and some skin cells turn cancerous. We are now seeing a similar phenomenon with mild cumulative repetitive head trauma.

You do not have to be a professional athlete to suffer permanent cognitive damage from mild repetitive head trauma. Protective headgear is not just for children and professionals. We all need to use it when we are engaged in any activity that has a significant potential for head trauma.

So, what happens after the trauma occurs? Do you just shake your head and say, "Boy, I had my bell rung," and ignore it, or should you seek medical attention? How do you make that determination? Here are five critical areas that will help you decide if you should seek medical attention:

1. **COGNITIVE:** Is there any memory loss; decrease in concentration; or feeling confused, foggy, or hazy?

2. **EMOTIONAL:** Do you feel sad, irritable, apathetic, depressed, or down?

3. **PHYSICAL:** Are you experiencing a headache, head pressure, dizziness, decreased balance or

coordination, nausea, vomiting, or increased sensitivity to light or noise?

4. **UNUSUAL CHANGES:** Is there anything abnormal from your usual routine or how you normally feel? Are you unusually sleepy at a time of the day when you're usually wide awake, or are you wide awake at a time of the day when you are normally sleepy?

5. **UNEQUAL PUPIL DIAMETER:** If you see a significant difference in pupil size between the left and right eye after someone has sustained head trauma, they need a medical assessment— immediately. Unequal pupil diameter is a classic sign of traumatic brain injury.

The important thing to remember is that these changes do not necessarily follow an immediate timeline. They may not show up for three, four, or even five days after the initial trauma.

PHYSICAL INACTIVITY

This is the most important one of all. We are born with approximately one hundred billion brain cells, or neurons. We lose about sixty thousand to ninety thousand a day through natural attrition, which is about one per second. If you want to significantly increase this loss, physical inactivity is one of the most efficient means of doing so. You can speed up the loss even further if the physical inactivity occurs in the same monotonous environment. This is deadly for people who are shut-ins, going through long-term convalescence, or those in senior and old-age homes. Not only is there no physical activity, but they are in the same, unstimulating environment. It is not much better for those who go to work every day and then come home and sit in front of the same television, in the same room, for five or six hours a night, every night.

"THE MOST EFFECTIVE WAY
TO EXERCISE YOUR BRAIN
IS TO EXERCISE YOUR BODY."

—David Bardsley

CHAPTER 4

ESSENTIALS FOR YOUR COGNITIVE IMPROVEMENT

IF WE CHOOSE TO INCREASE our cognitive abilities at any stage in life, two things are necessary. First, we must increase and balance all of the neurotransmitters in our brains (dopamine, GABA, acetylcholine, serotonin, etc.). Some areas of our brains may be deficient in a particular neurotransmitter, while other areas may have an excess of the same neurotransmitters, so balancing neurotransmitters is crucial. Some areas may actually need less, not more. There are at least one hundred and twenty neurotransmitters that we know of, and we do not have a pill to increase each of those neurotransmitters. Even if we did, what would you do, take over a hundred pills a day?

Fortunately, there is good news. Study after study has repeatedly shown that there is only one known modality that will increase and balance not only one, two, or three neurotransmitters, but all one hundred and twenty. And no, it is not Prozac, Zoloft, or Ritalin. It is *vigorous physical activity*. Not a walk in the park or a stroll with the dog, but vigorous, break-a-sweat exercise. We do not yet understand how this works, but scientists are able to place probes into the brains of laboratory animals, force them to exercise, and measure the increase in dopamine, acetylcholine, serotonin, and the other neurotransmitters while the animal is exercising. They are also able to determine how long it takes for the level of those neurotransmitters to slowly go back down to their pre-exercise level after the animal stops exercising. Psychiatrists have understood this for decades. You would be hard-pressed to find a psychiatrist anywhere who would not tell you that if they could

just get their patients to engage in daily vigorous physical activity that probably 70 percent of them could do away with the medications altogether, and the other 30 percent could probably cut their medications in half.

By the time I entered school, I had developed a whole series of very peculiar behaviors. I blurted strange noises when I spoke, developed uncontrollable facial tics and head jerks. After every third step I would spin in a complete circle before continuing, and I struggled academically. My frightened parents took me from specialist to specialist seeking a diagnosis and cure. I was hospitalized at age seven and told I needed "a rest." The final stop was the child psychiatrist who told my parents I was "mildly retarded" and would never progress past the sixth grade. His recommendation was to remove me from school and enroll me in a special training program where I would learn some valuable life skills. My parents did not accept this diagnosis and made a decision that would forever change my life. From that day on, they promised there would be no more doctors, therapists, special schools, or medication of any kind. What there was instead was relentless support, encouragement, love, and physical

exercise. Lots and lots of daily physical activity. It would be many years before the mystery was solved and a correct diagnosis was made.

When I was diagnosed with an intellectual disability (ID) at age nine, my parents did not know anything about the brain or neurotransmitters. They had high school educations but were smart enough to recognize that whenever I engaged in daily vigorous physical activity, all of my symptoms improved: my Tourette's syndrome, OCD, and ADHD symptoms and my tics were reduced; my focus and concentration improved; and my grades in school started to go up. Vigorous physical activity was the glue that held my life together as a child, and I can assure you it is absolutely the glue that holds my life together as an adult. Without it, I would be incapable of writing this book. Whatever neurotransmitters my brain lacks, vigorous physical activity provides. What exercise does for your body physically is a side benefit and an added bonus; it is what exercise does for you *mentally* that is truly remarkable.

If physical activity came in pill form and could be patented, it would be heralded as the mental health wonder drug of all time. Make no doubt about this, how you feel, right at this moment, or at any given moment in time, is not determined by how many brain cells you have but by the delicate balance or imbalance of those neurotransmitters. Let me ask you this: How much better would you perform in school or at your job if you showed up for work every single day in a better mood? What effect would it have on the bottom line of a company if every single employee showed up every day in a better mood? The *International Journal of Workplace Health Management* reported a study carried out in a series of insurance companies in Great Britain. They asked for volunteers who currently were not exercising. The volunteers were asked to exercise for one hour a day, two days a week. They could choose the days they wanted to exercise and the type of exercise they wished to perform, as long as it was done before coming to work. At the end of every workday, whether they exercised or not, they were given a questionnaire. This is what the employees themselves reported on days they exercised:

- The employees themselves felt they had a 41 percent increase in their motivation to work.
- They reported a 21 percent increase in their concentration while working on a day that they exercised versus the day before or the day after when they did not.
- There was a 22 percent increase in the workload they finished on time.
- There was 25 percent decrease in the number of unscheduled breaks on exercise days.

When the experimenters measured the overall productivity, they found a 15 percent increase in productivity on the days the employees exercised versus the day before or the day after when they did not.

GROW MORE NEURONS

The second thing we need to do if we want to increase our cognitive abilities is to increase the number of neurons and other brain cells we have. The latest neuroscience proves this can be done. We are born with about one hundred billion neurons and we lose seventy thousand to ninety thousand a day. That is about one per second. These daily losses need to be replaced, which is something that was thought to be impossible up until 1998. We also need to increase the number of connections between the brain cells; we need more branches.

Think of a squirrel that is trying to travel from one side of the forest to the other. It does not want to run along the forest floor, because it will most likely be eaten by predators. The squirrel runs up a tree trunk and then along a branch and tries to jump to a branch on the next tree. However, the forest is not particularly healthy and dense. The trees are rather sparse and have few branches. The squirrel is unable to jump to a branch on the next tree, so it scurries back toward the trunk and tries another branch, but again it is too far from another tree branch. The squirrel tries a third branch and this time it successfully leaps to the next tree. It continues this pattern of trial and error over and over until it finally reaches the other side of the forest safely.

What if the forest was healthy and the trees were abundant and spaced tightly together with many branches? The squirrel could then run out on the first branch and jump immediately to the adjacent tree and keep going. It would repeat this and cross the forest much more quickly. The trees represent the neurons in your brain, and the tree branches are like the dendrites (branches) of the neuron. The squirrel represents the electrical impulse. The more neurons and the more branches, the faster the electrical impulse will travel through the brain (brain processing speed).

How do we grow new neurons with lots of branches (dendrites)? I like to use the analogy of a lawn. You have some nice fertile soil, and you spread grass seeds on it and then do nothing but wait. One by one those dormant grass seeds will germinate, and a new blade of grass will pop up. Eventually, they will become a lawn. Within two or three years that lawn will be as thick and rich as it is ever going to be, unless we do something to help it. What do we spread on the lawn to make it healthier?

The answer of course is *fertilizer*. The fertilizer does two things. First, it strengthens each existing blade of grass; it makes it healthier and more resistant to disease, insects, and drought; therefore, the individual blades of grass die off less frequently. The second thing that occurs is that soil contains millions and millions of dormant grass seeds that have been sitting there since the day you spread them. For whatever reason they never fulfilled their genetic potential by germinating

"

YOUR BRAIN IS LIKE A SEED; NOURISH AND CARE FOR IT, AND IT WILL BLOSSOM.

—David Bardsley

and becoming a new blade of grass. However, when the fertilizer comes into contact with those dormant grass seeds, they immediately germinate and start to grow into what they were genetically programmed to be, new blades of grass. The lawn becomes denser and richer than ever. It turns out that the same sort of thing happens in our brains.

Back in 1998, a group of behavioral researchers at the Salk Institute for Biological Studies at the University of California in San Diego were doing a series of behavioral experiments using genetically identical mice. One of the experiments in the series was to test the intelligence of the mice. This was done using a series of mazes. Much to the surprise of the researchers, they found that some of the mice were cleverer than others, and it did not seem to make any difference whether the mice were young, middle-aged, or old. The researchers thought to themselves, "This should not be, they should be the same." Remember what we said about intelligence? Fifty percent of intelligence is inherited—these were genetically identical mice; they had exactly the same genetic material. Fifty percent is environmental, meaning it is dependent on how rich and stimulating our environment is when we are very young. These mice were all brought up in the same laboratory, in the same size cages, and with the same number of mice in each cage; they were given the same water and the same food. Their intelligence should have been clearly equal, but it was not. Then, one of the researchers noticed that the cages were not absolutely identical. Some of the cages had running wheels and some did not. Like most rodents, mice simply love to run; they get on those wheels and they run and run for hours at a time. When they went back and looked at their data, sure enough, the smart mice came from the cages with running wheels. The mice were then sacrificed, and their brain tissues were examined under high-powered microscopes. For the first time, the researchers saw thousands and thousands of new brain cells.

For one hundred years, neuroscience taught that we were born with a definitive number of brain cells (about one hundred billion) and once a brain cell dies, it was gone forever. We grow new skin cells, bone cells, and intestinal cells every day, but we were taught that when a brain cell dies, it is gone forever. Now, they had clear proof in front of them that the old theory that had been taught in neuroscience for one hundred years is completely wrong. The researchers found that **we, in fact, can grow new brain cells, and we can grow them at any stage of life.**

A little more investigation revealed exactly how

this occurs. It turns out that humans, like the mice, have millions and millions of dormant *stem* cells in our brains, which have been there since our birth. For whatever reason, these stem cells never went on to fulfill their genetic potential to become new neurons. Perhaps they were not supposed to; perhaps in the great scheme of things, these dormant stem cells were purposely placed there for our use later in life or for some other purpose we have yet to understand. What

DIAGRAM OF A NEURON

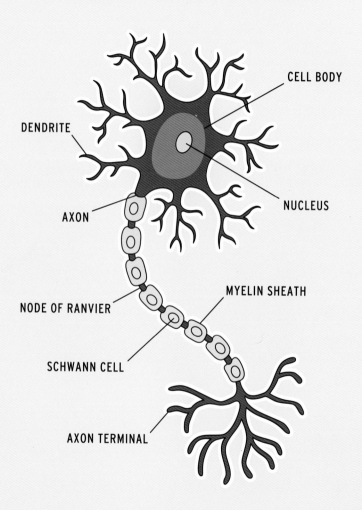

CELL BODY

DENDRITE

NUCLEUS

AXON

NODE OF RANVIER

MYELIN SHEATH

SCHWANN CELL

AXON TERMINAL

is amazing is that when these dormant stem cells come into contact with the fertilizer, they immediately start to differentiate and grow into new neurons. More neurons and more connections means better mental functioning. The fertilizer, it was discovered, is a polypeptide called brain-derived neurotrophic factor (BDNF). The mice could produce up to 200 percent more BDNF by running on the exercise wheels. So once again, vigorous physical activity was the key. We now understand exactly the sequence by which this occurs!

NEUROGENESIS

When we exercise vigorously, BDNF is released, which comes into contact with the dormant stem cells. The stem cells then start to fulfill their genetic potential and grow into a new neuron. More neurons mean better mental functioning.

Unfortunately, these animal experiments are very difficult to replicate in humans. Where are we going to find a group of humans that will allow us to force them into daily vigorous physical exercise, and then at the end of the experiment, sacrifice them so we can count the number of new brain cells? What evidence do we have that vigorous physical activity actually improves cognitive ability? Over the past forty or fifty years, there have been many studies performed, mainly with seniors and schoolchildren. The seniors were able to improve their cognitive abilities by initiating a daily exercise program. The studies also show that the more physically active the schoolchildren were, the better they performed academically at school. Studies have shown that children who ride the school bus perform worse on their academic tests than those who walk to school. The main problem with most of these studies is that they were small-scale studies. They involved one hundred students, five hundred seniors, fifteen hundred students, etc. However, in 2003 the California Department of Education wanted to know once and for all, "Is there a correlation between students' fitness levels and their overall academic achievement scores?"

They commissioned an enormous study—enormous in cost and magnitude. It involved almost one million students—884,714 to be exact—in the fifth, seventh, and ninth grades. Remember, it was previously believed that by the time a child was seven, eight, or a maximum of nine years of age, his or her intelligence was fixed and could not be improved. Even the youngest participants in this study, the seventh graders, were eleven years old. These are the results that were reported in the *Journal of Exercise Physiology* in February 2005: "As overall fitness scores improved, mean academic

achievement scores also improved."

But what about adults? My favorite study is the Swedish military study of 2009, which involved 1,240,000 military personnel of mixed ages. Here is their conclusion: "The higher the fitness level, the higher the cognition." The truly fascinating part of this study is that it included 1,400 sets of identical twins raised in the same environment. Remember what we said about intelligence: 50 percent is inherited. These twins possess exactly the same genetic material. Fifty percent of intelligence is developmental; meaning our intelligence is based on how stimulating our environment is when we are infants and very young children. These 1,400 sets of identical twins were raised in the same homes. Their intelligence should have been absolutely equal, and it was, as long as their fitness levels were equal. But when there was a significant difference in fitness levels, there was a significant difference in mental ability in the identical twins. *The more physically active the twin, the higher the mental acuity.*

Vigorous physical activity is obviously a key element to improving our cognitive abilities, but what type of physical activity? The following is a list of popular types of physical activity:

- Aerobic
- Balance
- Flexibility
- Strength
- Anaerobic
- Coordination

For your physical health, I would highly recommend all of these, but so far, the studies have shown that only aerobic, anaerobic, and strength exercises will lead to the cognitive increase we are looking for. The difference between aerobic and anaerobic is the intensity at which the exercises are done. If the activity is at a low enough intensity that you are able to take in a sufficient amount of oxygen to sustain the metabolic demands of your muscles and continue that activity for a prolonged time, it is considered an aerobic activity.

"

OUR MINDS HAVE THE INCREDIBLE CAPACITY TO BOTH ALTER THE STRENGTH OF CONNECTIONS AMONG NEURONS, ESSENTIALLY REWIRING THEM, AND CREATE ENTIRELY NEW PATHWAYS. IT MAKES A COMPUTER, WHICH CANNOT CREATE NEW HARDWARE WHEN ITS SYSTEM CRASHES, SEEM FIXED AND HELPLESS.

—Susannah Cahalan

"

If while performing the exact same activity you decide to increase the intensity, so that you are no longer able to take in enough oxygen to supply your metabolic demands, you have slipped over into the anaerobic phase.

Some of the newest studies are showing that even strength or resistance training can give us that same cognitive increase by balancing our neurotransmitters and promoting neurogenesis. The key factor is that these resistance exercises must be done with sufficient intensity that they significantly increase our heart rates. **This is crucial.** It is not the heart muscle itself that liberates the BDNF. Elevated heart rate is just an indication that our skeletal muscles are working hard enough. When the skeletal muscles are being stressed they release a hormone called insulin-like growth factor (ILGF) into the bloodstream, which then passes the blood–brain barrier and stimulates the brain cells to release more BDNF—the fertilizer for the stem cells.

THE CRITICAL KEY: HEART RATE

When we are exercising, it is difficult to maintain our heart rates at a specific level, so we look for a range with an upper and lower limit and try to keep our heart rate within the Target Heart Rate (THR) or ideal range while exercising. The best method for determining your THR is calculated through your Resting Heart Rate (RHR). Simply count your heart rate (pulse) for one full minute. Once you have the Beats Per Minute (BPM) you can calculate your THR using the following formula.

The example below is for a sixty-five-year-old with a RHR of 50. Substitute your age and RHR into this formula to determine your Target Heart Rate.

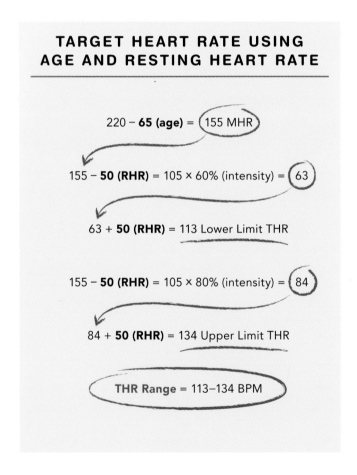

TARGET HEART RATE USING AGE AND RESTING HEART RATE

220 − **65 (age)** = (155 MHR)

155 − **50 (RHR)** = 105 × 60% (intensity) = (63)

63 + **50 (RHR)** = 113 Lower Limit THR

155 − **50 (RHR)** = 105 × 80% (intensity) = (84)

84 + **50 (RHR)** = 134 Upper Limit THR

THR Range = 113–134 BPM

HOW TO GET STARTED AND INCREASE YOUR ACTIVITY TODAY

OBTAIN A HEART MONITOR BEFORE YOU START TO EXERCISE

If you are not currently exercising, don't dive in quite yet. Just get the heart monitor and wear it every day for one full week, from the time you get up until you go to bed. Note the roller coaster ride your heart rate takes during the day. We all expect our heart rates to increase if we run or walk up a flight of stairs, but you can see what effect the food you eat or beverages you drink will have on your heart rate, what effect having a difficult conversation with someone will have on your heart rate, and how your emotions affect your heart rate. If you are like most, you will find yourself almost addicted to continuously checking your heart rate. If you already have an exercise program, then the heart rate monitor will take you to the next level very quickly.

CHOOSE YOUR ACTIVITIES

The more activities in your repertoire, the easier it will be to succeed, and you will not suffer from boredom or repetitive strain injuries. Once you choose them, get some help in performing the activity correctly. Unless you participated in that sport or activity at an elite level earlier in your life, get some help getting started, so that you are performing the activity properly and do not injure yourself. Even if it is something as simple as running. I can guarantee you if you just pull those old running shoes out of the closet and start pounding the pavement, in no time at all you will have shin splints, knee pain, or hip pain, and you are going to quit. Always seek expert advice!

What if you have never exercised but you want to be smarter next year? I have spoken to audiences where people tell me they have never been athletic, and they have no idea what activity they should try. This method may help you decide: most people have a favorite cause or charity. Almost all charities today have some

sort of athletic event to raise money. Find out what that event is for your favorite charity, and then work toward participating in the event (with expert advice and proper equipment). You are not only helping yourself, but you will be motivated by the higher cause. If all else fails and you cannot find an activity that appeals to you, then simply pick one and challenge yourself, and your brain will thank you.

SCHEDULE TIME

If you are not currently involved in a physical activity program, start with committing to three times a week. The critical factor for success here is that you must schedule the time beforehand. Look at your schedule for the upcoming week and set aside the time that you are going to perform your chosen activity or activities. Enter it as a time block; do not let anyone schedule anything else at that time. It is a date you cannot break. It is preferable if you are able to perform the activity at the same time on each of those three days, because this sets up habits. If you decide you are going to exercise on Tuesdays, Thursdays, and Saturdays, and you wake up on Tuesday morning and have no idea when you are going to perform the activity that day, the chance of you doing it before you go to bed that night is basically zero. Do not kid yourself; unless you schedule it, it is not going to happen.

I have sat in the audience countless times and listened to fitness experts on the stage and they all say the same thing: "Look, we are all busy, from the time we get up in the morning to the time we go to bed; the solution is simple. Just set the damn alarm clock thirty or forty minutes earlier each day and get up and get it done." That is probably the worst advice you could possibly follow. We just discussed how critically important sleep is to your cognitive ability. The last thing I want to see you do is rob yourself of thirty or forty minutes of that critical sleep time to try to jam in some physical exercise. What you might gain cognitively from the exercise you are going to lose by the sleep deprivation, so you will be no further ahead. If you do decide to get up early and do your exercise first thing in the morning, then you must go to bed that much earlier the night before, so you still have that necessary seven to nine hours of sleep.

FIND FRIENDS

Once you choose your activity or activities, it is critically important to try to find others to do it with you.

"EXERCISE HAS A PROFOUND
IMPACT ON COGNITIVE ABILITIES
AND MENTAL HEALTH. IT IS SIMPLY
ONE OF THE BEST TREATMENTS WE
HAVE FOR PSYCHIATRIC PROBLEMS."

—John J. Ratey

Encourage friends to accompany you. It may not be possible to have the same people accompany you each time you exercise, so try to arrange to have different people participate in the activity with you on different days. If you cannot find friends to do it with you, then you can join a group. If you can get other people to participate in the activity with you, your success rate skyrockets. A number of years ago, *Runner's World* published the results of a very interesting long-term study. Even though they were talking about runners, I believe we can extrapolate and apply this to any type of exercise. They divided runners into four categories:

1. **The Competitor:** This is the person who likes to compete against other athletes or compete against themselves by running against the clock.

2. **The Exerciser:** This person does not particularly enjoy exercising. When the alarm goes off at 5:30 a.m., they think; "It's cold, it's dark, it's

raining. I don't want to do this." However, they know it is good for them mentally and good for them physically, and they know they will feel better afterward. They force themselves out of bed, put on their gear, and away they go. They always feel better afterward.

3. **The Enthusiast:** This person just genuinely enjoys some aspect of the physical activity. Perhaps it is the mountain biker who does not care about their speed, distance, or cadence. They just thoroughly enjoy riding their bike along the path through the woods beside the beautiful stream. They are enthused about some aspect of their ride.

4. **The Socializer:** This is the person who shows up for the activity primarily for the social interaction. The mental and physical benefits are secondary.

Their long-term study showed that the competitor and the exerciser fall by the wayside. Those who do it for a long time, and a lifetime, are the enthusiast and the socializer. So whatever activities you choose, grab a friend and try to find activities that will help you fall into one of those two categories to help ensure your long-term success!

CLOTHING AND EQUIPMENT

When it comes to clothing and equipment, there is just one rule: buy good quality. If you have good quality equipment, you will enjoy the activity more and if you enjoy it, you will engage in that activity more frequently. If you decide to start cycling, please do not resurrect that forty-year-old bicycle that has been rusting in your basement for decades and weighs ninety-five pounds. You do not have to buy a five-thousand-dollar carbon fiber racing bike to get started, but you will need to spend four hundred to five hundred dollars to buy a decent bicycle that you will enjoy and want to use

frequently. Without enjoyment, you may be able to force yourself to do the activity because you know that it is good for you, but it will not be sustainable over the long term; you will eventually quit.

When it comes to clothing, clothing is equipment. Today's clothing is so highly technical and functional it is absolutely considered part of your equipment. The Norwegians have a wonderful saying, "There is no such thing as bad weather, there is just bad clothing." They are absolutely correct. If you choose to exercise outdoors, you should be able to do so in any climatic condition and stay dry, warm, and comfortable or cool, dry, and comfortable—if you have the proper clothing. And while you are shopping, why not buy clothing that looks good on you? You need every psychological lift possible, because we are talking about doing this for a lifetime, not a short time. Good clothing and equipment will make any physical activity more enjoyable.

SIX OR SEVEN DAYS A WEEK

All of the latest studies show that thirty minutes a day of vigorous physical activity is sufficient to promote neurogenesis (the growth of new brain cells) and balance our neurotransmitters. Longer is better but the biggest gain occurs in the first thirty minutes. There is both good news and bad news here. I am going to give you the good news first. Within ten minutes of you engaging in vigorous physical activity, there will be a significant increase of all your neurotransmitters (dopamine, acetylcholine, serotonin, etc.).

The bad news is that as soon as you stop exercising, those neurotransmitters will slowly decrease back to their original pre-exercise levels. This decrease will take six to sixteen hours to occur. This is why it is important to exercise six or seven days a week. Alternatively, you do not have to exercise every day if you do not want to, just exercise on the days you want to be smarter. I am often asked; "Is there a particular time of the day that it is better to exercise?" That depends on your schedule. I try to exercise first thing in the morning, because I want my neurotransmitters to be elevated to their peak levels during the day when I am using my brain more actively and when my mood and attitude matter the most. I do not think that exercising in the evening will be as significant a benefit to me mentally. Perhaps I may have more clever dreams, but that is about it. People often say we need to rest at least one day a week. We do not. Professional athletes certainly do because they stress their bodies to a degree that we cannot even imagine. They require a day of rest each week to allow their bodies to repair the damaged tissue. You are not trying to push your body to the point of stress but rather healthfully engage in a physical activity each and every day.

The good news is that the new neurons that you develop through physical exercise will hopefully last you the rest of your life, or at least for decades to come; that is the long-term benefit of vigorous daily exercise.

RETEST

If you were trying to lose twenty pounds, and two weeks later you got on the scale and you saw you were down thirteen pounds, how would that make you feel? You would be encouraged, would you not? When you see the improvement and that you are moving in the right direction that will encourage you to continue.

Remember, we are following this action plan to help improve our cognitive abilities and we would like to see results. You might notice that your memory or your recall for faces or names is improving, but often the improvement occurs gradually, and we do not notice it. That is why it is good to test yourself and then retest yourself every five or six months. Once you see the improvement occurring you will find it easier to continue, and you will not want to slide back and lose ground. Success begets success. You can go to the website davidbardsley.com and click on the "online learning" tab. Each month you will be sent a free, self-scored cognitive test. Keep track of your monthly scores to monitor your progress.

EIGHT STEPS TO MAKE YOU SMARTER

WE HAVE SPOKEN A GREAT deal about the remarkable effects of physical activity on your cognitive ability, but do not forget the other factors we discussed. There is no single "magic bullet" to becoming smarter next year. You need to address all of these factors at the same time. This shotgun approach will ensure that you experience the maximum cognitive improvement in the shortest time. You can do this. Yes, it takes some effort and some willpower, but the results are well worth it today and for many years to come. It is the gift that keeps on giving.

1. **Improve sleep:** Improving sleep is one of the easiest methods to ensure you are functioning at your maximum cognitive ability. Tonight, follow the four simple suggestions discussed on pages 44–48, and you will improve the quality and quantity of your sleep.

2. **Eliminate toxic exposures:** Look around your home and workplace and remove all toxic materials. Read labels carefully, and follow instructions on using the products safely. This includes household cleaning products.

3. **Manage mental health:** Do not ignore stress, anxiety, or depression and think they will pass on their own. Seek professional help, and you will get over them or learn how to manage their symptoms much faster and return to a happier, healthier you.

4. **Assess drugs:** Work with your physician to reduce or eliminate all possible medications. Read the warnings on all drug packaging (even over-the-counter medications) and heed any warnings.

5. **Eat a well-rounded diet and take vitamins:** Have your vitamin B12 levels checked if you are taking proton pump inhibitors on a daily basis (Nexium, Prilosec, Prevacid, etc). Preventing vitamin deficiencies is easier than reversing them.

6. **Limit alcohol:** You do not have to abstain from alcohol, but try to keep daily consumption to no more than one ounce of spirits, three ounces of wine, or one beer in any given day.

7. **Protect your head:** Wear protective headgear when participating in any risky activity.

8. **Stay active:** Daily vigorous physical activity is the single most effective means of improving and maintaining optimum cognitive ability. Make it fun, and you will reap the incredible benefits.

"OUR BRAINS RENEW
THEMSELVES THROUGHOUT
LIFE TO AN EXTENT
PREVIOUSLY THOUGHT
NOT POSSIBLE."

—Michael S. Gazzaniga

EPILOGUE

OTHER THAN SOME UP-TO-DATE SCIENTIFIC information, there is nothing new about the core principle that daily vigorous physical exercise will make you smarter next year. Five thousand years ago, one of the greatest civilizations of all time, the Greeks, rose to world prominence based on a very simple principle.

"Νοῦς ὑγιὴς ἐν σώματι ὑγιεῖ"

You all know this principle, you have heard it thousands of times. *A sound mind in a sound body.* Few of us live our lives guided by this principle. We do not follow it anymore—why not?

Each one of you is a leader in your own particular way, and the one characteristic that all leaders share is that they lead by example. Whether you want to accept the responsibility or not, you exert great influence on those around you, on your family, friends, coworkers, etc. Whenever they see you do anything to improve yourself, whether it is mentally, physically, or spiritually, they will want to follow and do the same. You may take on a program like this to improve your own cognitive ability, but without even knowing it, you will influence those around you to do the same, and you will help elevate them to a higher level of existence with improved cognitive ability, and for that, I honor you.

My parents understood that, and this is how the story ended from all those years ago with the psychiatrist that told them I was hopeless. When I was first starting out as a practicing maxillofacial surgeon and had just opened my new surgery clinic, my father called me at my new office.

"Hi, Dad. How are you? What's going on?" I asked.

"Dave, I was wondering, do you have your business cards printed yet?"

"I do. Actually, I think they just came in last week. Why?"

"I was wondering if you would send me some, I would like one hundred."

"What! One hundred? Are you sure?"

"Yep, one hundred, please."

"Well, OK, if that's what you want."

We said our goodbyes, and as I hung up the phone, I thought, *How proud my parents must be at the way things have turned out, that my father wants one hundred of my business cards to hand out to his friends and acquaintances.* A wonderful warm feeling welled up inside me.

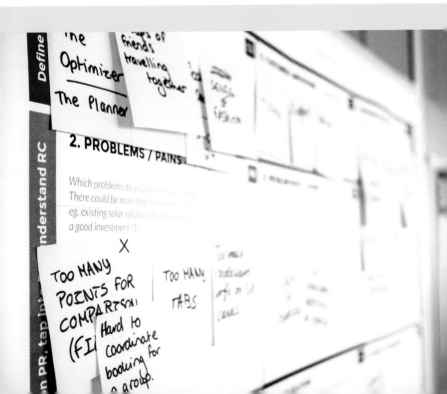

The years passed, and it was not until five years after my father's death that I learned the fate of those one hundred business cards. Several months before my father was forced to close the old family hat business, he took what little money he had left and purchased a small insurance agency, which was located in a small two-story building. The insurance agency occupied the second floor, and there were two small offices on the ground floor that were rented to commercial tenants. Not long after, my father acquired the property and he recognized the name on one of the rental office doors. It was the same child psychiatrist who had diagnosed me as "mentally retarded" twenty-two years before.

For one hundred days, my father barged into the psychiatrist's office, planted himself in front of his desk, reached into his pocket, took out one of my business cards, held it up in front of the psychiatrist and said, "By the way, my son, the *'retarded'* maxillofacial surgeon, is doing juuust fine. Thanks for asking." He threw the card on the desk, turned, and swaggered out.

"

ANY MAN COULD, IF HE WERE
SO INCLINED, BE THE
SCULPTOR OF HIS OWN BRAIN.

—Santiago Ramón y Cajal

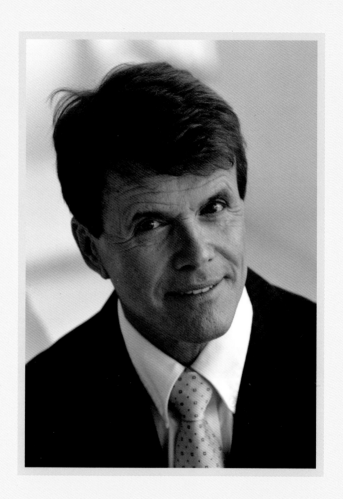

ABOUT THE AUTHOR

DR. DAVID C. BARDSLEY IS a bubbling cauldron of optimism, intellectual curiosity, and exuberance. But it wasn't always that way. David's was a troubled childhood, punctuated by years of intensive medical investigation, a period of institutionalization, and a misdiagnosis of an intellectual disability (ID) by the time he was nine years old.

Fortunately, it was a diagnosis his parents refused accept. They supported him, encouraged him, and challenged him to achieve what doctors said would be impossible. Eventually their mantra, "We believe in you," became his mantra, "I believe in me."

This is a remarkable story of perseverance and the unconditional support of loving parents. It was not easy; he would struggle with his dysfunctional behavior for nearly two decades before a correct diagnosis of Tourette's syndrome and ADHD was made, but he would go on to earn a BS, MS, DDS, and a fellowship in oral and maxillofacial surgery.

Today, David carries that passion for self-actualization into every part of his life. He is deeply passionate about the benefits of education and our ability to shape our own destiny when it comes to the quality of our lives.

He is the founder of Silver Eagle Media, a company dedicated to helping individuals increase their cognitive abilities and perform at their highest intellectual level. He spends most of his time crisscrossing the continent presenting his message to business executives, teachers, parents, and students.

RECOMMENDED READING

Ali, T., D. N. Roberts, W. M. Tierney. "Long-Term Safety
   Concerns with Proton Pump Inhibitors." *The American
   Journal of Medicine* Vol. 122, no. 10 (2009).

Amen, Daniel. *A Magnificent Brain at Any Age.* Harmony
   Books, 2009.

Amen, Daniel. *Change your Brain, Change Your Body.* Three
   Rivers Press, 2010.

Axelrad, D. A., D. C. Bellinger, L. M. Ryan. "Dose-Response
   Relationship of Prenatal Mercury Exposure and IQ:
   An Integrative Analysis of Epidemiologic Data."
   Environmental Health Perspective April, no. 115 (2007).

Barkhoudarian, G., D. A. Hovda, C. C. Giza. "The Molecular

Pathophysiology of Concussive Brain Injury." *Clinics in Sports Medicine* Vol. 30, no. 1 (2011).

Baverman, Eric. *The Edge Effect*. Sterling Publishing, 2005.

Baverman, Eric. *Younger Brain, Sharper Mind*. Rodale Books, 2013.

Brizendine, Louanne. *The Female Brain*. Broadway Books, 2007.

Brizendine, Louanne. *The Male Brain*. Three Rivers Press, 2011.

Churchill, J. D., R. Galvez, S. Colcombe, R. A. Swain. "Exercise, Experience, and the Aging Brain." *Neurobiology of Aging* Vol. 23, no. 5 (2002).

Clarke, R., J. Birks, E. Nexo, P. M. Ueland. "Low Vitamin B-12 Status and Risk of Cognitive Decline in Older Adults." *American Journal of Clinical Nutrition* Vol. 86, no. 5 (2007).

Clarkson-Smith, L., A. A. Hartley. "Relationships between Physical Exercise and Cognitive Abilities in Older Adults." *Psychology and Aging* Vol. 4, no. 2 (1989).

Colcombe, S. J., K. I. Erickson. "Aerobic Exercise Training

Increases Brain Volume in Aging Humans." *Journals of Gerontology* Vol. 61, no. 11 (2006).

Coyle, Daniel. *The Talent Code*. Bantam Books, 2009.

Dahl, R. E. "The Impact of Inadequate Sleep on Children's Daytime Cognitive Function." *Seminars in Pediatric Neurology* Vol. 3, no. 1 (1996).

Deford, S. M., M. S. Wilson, A. C. Rice. "Repeated Mild Brain Injuries Result in Cognitive Impairment in B6C3F1 Mice." *Journal of Neurotrauma* Vol 19, no. 4 (2002).

Den Elzen, W. P. J., Y. Groeneveld. "Long-Term Use of Proton Pump Inhibitors and Vitamin B12 Status in Elderly Individuals." *Alimentary Pharmacology & Therapeutics* Vol. 27, no. 6 (2008).

Doldge, Norman. *The Brain That Changes Itself*. Penguin Books, 2007.

Drummond, S. P. A., G. G. Brown. "The Effects of Total Sleep Deprivation on Cerebral Responses to Cognitive Performance." *Neuropsychopharmacology* Vol. 25, no. 5 (2001).

Dweck, Carol. *Mindset: The New Psychology of Success*.

Ballantine Books, 2008.

Fields, Douglas. *The Other Brain*. Simon & Schuster, 2011.

Gleick, J. *Faster: The Acceleration of Just About Everything.*
Phantom Books, 1999.

Grandjean, P., P. Weihe, R. F. White, F. Debes. "Cognitive
Performance of Children Prenatally Exposed to 'Safe
Levels of Methylmercury.'" *Environmental Research* Vol.
77, no. 2 (1998).

Guskiewicz, K. M., S. W. Marshall, J. Bailes, M. McCrea.
"Association between Recurrent Concussion and
Late-Life Cognitive Impairment in Retired Professional
Football Players." *Journal of Neurosurgery* Vol 27, no. 4
(2005).

Harrison, Y., J. A. Horne. "One Night of Sleep Loss Impairs
Innovative Thinking and Flexible Decision Making."
Organizational Behavior and Human Decision Processes
Vol. 78, no. 2 (1999).

Henderson, R., and C. Murray. *The Bell Curve*. Free Press
Paperbacks, 1996.

Hillman, C. H., K. I. Erickson, A. F. Kramer. "Be Smart,

Exercise Your Heart: Exercise Effects on Brain and Cognition." *Nature* Vol. 9 (2008).

Howden, C. W., "Vitamin B12 Levels During Prolonged Treatment with Proton Pump Inhibitors." *Journal of Clinical Gastroenterology* Vol. 30, no. 1 (2000).

Jacobson, J. L., S. W. Jacobson, R. J. Padgett. "Effects of Prenatal PCB Exposure on Cognitive Processing Efficiency and Sustained Attention." *Developmental Psychology* Vol. 28, no. 2 (1992).

Jorm, A. F. "Is Depression a Risk Factor for Dementia or Cognitive Decline?" *Gerontology* Vol. 46 (2000).

Lam, J. R., J. L. Schneider, W. Zhao, D. A. Corley. "Proton Pump Inhibitor and Histamine 2 Receptor Antagonist Use and Vitamin B12 Deficiency." *JAMA* Vol. 310, no. 22 (2013).

Laurer, H. L., F. M. Bareyre, V. M. Lee. "Mild Head Injury Increasing the Brain's Vulnerability to a Second Concussive Impact." *Journal of Neurosurgery* Vol. 95, no. 5 (2001).

Lewis, M., J. Worobey, D. S. Ramsay, M. K. McCormack.

"Prenatal Exposure to Heavy Metals: Effect on Childhood Cognitive Skills and Health Status." *Pediatrics* Vol. 89, no. 6 (1992).

Lim, J., D. F. Dinges. "A Meta-Analysis of the Impact of Short-Term Sleep Deprivation on Cognitive Variables." *Psychological Bulletin* Vol. 136, May (2010).

Lipton, Bruce. *The Biology of Belief*. Hay House Publishing, 2007.

Louv, Richard. *Last Child in the Woods*. Algonquin Books, 2008.

Lundy-Ekmann, Laurie. *Neuroscience: Fundamentals for Rehabilitation*. Saunders, 2012.

Magavi, S. S., B. R. Leavitt, and J. D. Macklis, "Induction of Neurogenesis in the Cortex of Adult Mice," *Nature* 405, June (2000).

McEwan, Bruce. *The End of Stress as We Know It*. Dana Press, 2012.

McKee, A. C., R. C. Cantu, C. J. Nowinski. "Chronic Traumatic Encephalopathy in Athletes: Progressive Tauopathy Following Repetitive Head Injury." *Journal of*

Neuropathology Vol. 68, no. 7 (2009).

Medina, John. *Brain Rules*. Pear Press, 2014.

Milman, A., A. Rosenberg, R. Weizman, "Mild Traumatic Brain Injury Induces Persistent Cognitive Deficits and Behavioral Disturbances in Mice." *Journal of Neurotrauma* Vol. 22, no. 9 (2005).

Nassir, Ghaemi. *A First-Rate Madness*. Penguin Press, 2011.

Neeper, S. A., F. G. Gomez-Pinilla, J. Chois, C. W. Cotman, "Physical Activity Increases mRNA for Brain-Derived Neurotropic Factor and Nerve Growth Factor in Rat Brain." *Brain Research* Vol. 726, no. 1 (1996).

Oken, E., R. O. Wright, K. P. Kleinman, D. Bellinger. "Maternal Fish Consumption, Hair Mercury, and Infant Cognition in a U.S. Cohort." *Environmental Health Perspectives* Vol. 113, no. 10 (2005).

Oliff, H. S., N. C. Berchtold, P. Isackson, and C. W. Cotman. "Exercise-Induced Regulation of Brain-Derived Neurotrophic Factor (BNDF) Transcripts in the Rat Hippocampus." *Brain Research* Vol. 61, no. 1 (1998).

Patandin, S., C. I. Lanting, P. G. H. Mulder, E. R. Boersma.

"Effects of Environmental Exposure to Polychlorinated Biphenyls and Dioxins on Cognitive Abilities in Dutch Children at 42 Months of Age." *Journal of Pediatrics* Vol. 134, no. 1 (1999).

Pawlak, R., B. S. S. Rao, J. P. Melchor. "Tissue Plasminogen Activator and Plasminogen Mediate Stress-Induced Decline of Neuronal and Cognitive Functions in the Mouse Hippocampus." *Proceedings of the National Academy of Sciences* Vol. 102, no. 50 (2005).

Pearlmutter, David. *Grain Brain.* Little, Brown and Company, 2013.

Peavy, G. M., D. P. Salmon, M. W. Jacobson. "Effects of Chronic Stress on Memory Decline in Cognitively Normal and Mildly Impaired Older Adults." *American Journal of Psychiatry* Vol. 166, no. 12 (2009).

Pilcher, J. J., A. S. Walters. "How Sleep Deprivation Affects Psychological Variables Related to College Students' Cognitive Performance." *Journal of American College Health* Vol. 46, no. 3 (1997).

Pink, Daniel H. *A Whole New Mind.* Penguin Books, 2006.

Pink, Daniel H. *Drive*. Penguin Books, 2011.

Ratey, John. *Spark: The New Science of Exercise and the Brain*. Little, Brown and Company, 2008.

Samkoff, J. S., C. H. Jacques. "A Review of Studies Concerning Effects of Sleep Deprivation and Fatigue on Residents' Performance." *Academic Medicine* Vol. 66, no. 11 (1991).

Sax, Lenard. *Boys Adrift*. Basic Books, 2009.

Selhub, J., L. C. Bagley, J. Miller. "B Vitamins, Homocysteine, and Neurocognitive Function in the Elderly." *American Journal of Clinical Nutrition* Vol. 71, no. 2 (2000).

Sood, Amit. *Log On: Two Steps to Mindful Awareness*. Morning Dew Publications, 2009.

Sood, Amit. *The Mayo Clinic Guide to Stress-Free Living*. Da Capo Press, 2013.

Steffens, D. C., E. Otey. "Perspectives on Depression, Mild Cognitive Impairment, and Cognitive Decline." *Archives of Psychiatry* Vol. 63, no. 2 (2006).

Stern, R. A., D. O. Riley, D. H. Daneshvar, C. J. Nowinski. "Long-Term Consequences of Repetitive Brain Trauma:

Chronic Traumatic Encephalopathy." *PM&R* Vol. 3, no. 10 (2011).

Swan, G. E., C. N. Lessov-Schlaggar. "The Effects of Tobacco Smoke and Nicotine on Cognition and the Brain." *Neuropsychology Review* Vol. 17, no. 3 (2007).

Sweeney, Michael. *Brain Works*. National Geographic, 2011.

Talbott, Shawn. *The Cortisol Connection*. Hunter House, 2002.

Tomporowski, P. D., N. R. Ellis. "Effects of Exercise on Cognitive Processes: A Review." *Psychological Bulletin* Vol. 99, no. 3 (1986).

van Praag, H., G. Kempermann, and F. H. Cage. "Running Increases Cell Proliferation and Neurogenesis in the Adult Mouse Dentate Gyrus." *Neuroscience* Vol. 2 (1999).

Vaynman, S., F. Gomez-Pinilla. "License to Run: Exercise Impacts Functional Plasticity in the Intact and Injured Central Nervous System by Using Neurotrophins." *Neurorehabilitation and Neural Repair* (2005).

Vaynman, S., Z. Ying. "Hippocampal BDNF Mediates

the Efficacy of Exercise on Synaptic Plasticity and Cognition." *European Journal of Neuroscience* (2004).

Williamson, A. M., A. M. Feyer. "Moderate Sleep Deprivation Produces Impairments in Cognitive and Motor Performance Equivalent to Legally Prescribed Levels of Alcohol Intoxication." *Occupational and Environmental Medicine* Vol. 57, no. 10 (2000).

Wilson, J., and J. Wright. *Adrenal Fatigue.* Smart Publications, 2001.

Yaffe, K., D. Barnes, M. Nevitt. "A Prospective Study of Physical Activity and Cognitive Decline in Elderly Women: Women Who Walk." *Archives of Internal Medicine* Vol. 161, no. 14 (2001).